Teach Anger Management Now

(COOLANGER TM)

By

Joseph D. Hayes

Table of Contents

Chapter 1 The counselor/teacher and qualities:

Chapter 2 How to start an anger management program.

Chapter 3 What is needed for anger management program

Chapter 4 Dealing with Adolescent Anger Management.

Chapter 5 The Cool Anger model of Anger Management (Origin and Faulty Beliefs)

Chapter 6 Cool Anger model continued (change viewed from a counselors view)

Chapter 7 Cool Anger model continued (Happiness= True Meaning and Purpose)

Chapter 8 Cool Anger model (What is Anger?)

Chapter 9 Letting Go, Forgiveness and shedding the labels

Forward

Creation of the Cool Anger Management Program

Joseph D. Hayes is a licensed counselor in the state of Texas. He has five years experience under his belt working with the criminal justice population at an Out-Patient Substance Abuse clinic called Crossroads Council on Alcohol and Drug Abuse. It was at this location that Joseph began his studies involving clients with angry related issues.

He attended many CEUs workshops on anger management and finally attended a TACADA workshop where he received his Instructor Certificate of Certification for the Anger Management "RETHINK" Program. He then compiled various bits and pieces of his educational notes and successfully blended them with several theories in what he perceived as essential and pragmatic rules for working with the angry client.

Mr. Hayes has developed a model called "Cool Anger" which combines education, awareness, insight, cognitive and real life applications to provide the client with the proper self empowerment to initiate changes within himself. Joseph feels that it is important that the client chooses to change his behavior and thinking on his own terms.

Mr. Hayes believes angry reactions are a type of learned behavior and incorporates thoughts which are utilized as a coping mechanism in the client's life development. Since the client is now aged and matured these coping skills prove to be no longer necessary nor useful to the client and must be eliminated. Usually the client will identify himself as having self destructive beliefs and experiences which the program attempts to redirect into a positive self growth. Mr. Hayes has taught this approach for six years in Hunt County for both the criminal and civil courts system.

Joseph Hayes has experienced tremendous positive responses from his cliental and has records which indicate how they have successfully utilized the principles found in this program to get their life back on the proper track.

Today, Mr. Hayes continues to teach anger management and operates a small private practice in Mount Pleasant. He has developed this online course with the very same objectives and material that he has used successfully with his cliental.

To his credit Joseph Hayes has several recommendations including one from the former County Attorney Keith Willaford exclaiming the benefits of Mr. Hayes' Anger management Program. In today's high technology world learning Anger Management via the internet can be more convenient and cost effective of a method then doing so in person.

Naturally, you will readily find many who will shun any type of education completed over the web, but the fact remains that today many people are receiving wholesome and beneficial education over the World Wide Web.

Such programs as the Kids First Program, Defensive Driving and even many certified college degrees are effectively completed online. These various programs have met with huge success and I feel this program will satisfy any skeptic if they are open to viewing and participating in the enclosed course. People will only get what they are willing to invest in an educational class whether that course is offered in person or online.

Being a counselor has allowed me to fully understand this dramatic notion. In my years of working in the subject area I have met with resistance on a daily basis in solicitation of the idea involving anger management instructions online. One individual expressed to me her concerns that those clients who take the live version of this course get something therapeutic from the interaction with other clients in the class. She, like others, perceived anger management as treatment. Anger Management is education that can have therapeutic value, but I would like to stress that it is not treatment and has never been considered treatment.

Unfortunately, this lady was not looking at reality since her thoughts were that by merely attending and interacting with others in class the students would automatically benefit from the interaction. I have had clients sleep while attending my class, claim that they are there only because the courts said they must attend and others who proved to be extremely disruptive. During the presentations they have resisted any sort of change and several have even engaged in heated verbal altercations which was accompanied by potentially trouble seeking behavior. Often times these types of behaviors will sabotage the learning of others and must be dealt with properly. So as you can readily see you will get what you ultimately put into this program.

Your goal should ultimately be to possess the power to change yourself as no one else can do that for you. Here is your opportunity to prove to yourself and to others that you can change and grow for the better.

Chapter 1

"It takes a special person to be an anger management Instructor."

I can vividly recall those days when I was actively employed with the Crossroads Council on Alcohol and Drug Abuse. I continually took delight in working with the angry resistant clients as I found the experience to be extremely challenging. As I gained further experience in proper guidance of these people I watched intensively as the patients themselves made vast improvements in there attitudes. Naturally, there were those occasional tough cases which would challenge me to the end of my wits; however, throughout the complete experience I was able to establish a viable program that worked successfully for most of my clients. In addition, I recall watching many of the other "Know it all" counselors as they lost their cool manner and often went bonkers when dealing with these clients. In this book I would like to discuss and qualify what I believe creates a good anger management instructor. No discussion could be complete without expressing adequate information on those points which hamper an individual's progress as well.

I started my career working with an Intensive drug outpatient group which fell under the control of the probation department, the various courts, and of course the counseling center. As I attended many CEU workshops, I soon discovered that many of them would explained the origins of the patients anger, they would recount any biological influences which would effect their actions and eventually how to identify such behavior. At the conclusion of these sessions I would always leave with a great insight into the fundamentals involved but completely lacked the specific understandings on exactly how to deal and treat those condition which are not in the DSM4. I was fortunate enough to become certified by TACADA in the area of an experimental anger management program called "RETHINK". I found this to be a very effective program as it was family orientated and was a highly developmentally education implemented curriculum.

At this point in time I was fully certified as an Anger Management Specialist. Under my belt, I had several successfully completed CEUs and had completed the certification program. Although all this advanced education was a counselors blessing I discovered that I achieved much better results in my therapy sessions by using a combination of three major theories, *Gestalt theory, Person*

Centered and Existentialism. These theories were gracefully combined in order to meet the client's demands in their struggle to overcome their anger reactions. I would like at this time to break these theories up into a normal order of usages.

The Gestalt theory is used primarily to assist the client in gaining an awareness that his current manner of behavior has not worked and that all his choices whether they be good or bad has left him living in his present consequences. At this point I am talking confrontation which would challenge the client to adequately process his/her present situation in a logical and factual manner. You must never confront the client in a quarrelsome manner. Keep in mind that generally the clients are usually well guarded in their attitudes and possibly possess much better argumentative skills then displayed by the instructor. With this thought in mind you will find it better that the client challenge himself rather than for the instructor to challenge him/her. As an example, suppose a client may state that;

"She made me so mad that I couldn't stop from hitting her".

Great confrontation has to be learned or acquired so at first allow me to give you the wrong type of confrontational response with an included explanation. The wrong Counselor response would be,

"Sounds like your blaming someone else for your responsibility".

Naturally this fact may probably be true however, I believe this would automatically initiate a defensive response as well as an agitated feeling from the client. It is likely that it would also generate negative projections onto the image of the therapist/instructor from the clients' viewpoint. At that point, you may very well have lost the client for he/she is more then likely waiting for you to say something controversy to which they can argue with you about. To fully appreciate this point you must become aware of where the client is coming from as most have had altercations with authority figures previously so with the confrontation you present you merely struck a nerve which allowed the client to project his past experience onto you as the instructor. Actually a much better qualitative therapeutic confrontation intervention would be,

"It seems that you allowed someone you care about to effectively push your buttons until you did something that you regret, as it is obvious your values disagree with what you did."

Now hopefully I have just demonstrated an un-judgmental empathy that possibly got the clients attention while permitting him to be more accepting of my future teachings while in the class. I do not wish to project the image that I am against the client as my goal in the class is to become an ally with the client and empower him/her to set their path towards achieving change. After the above confrontation I would immediately follow up with;

"Are you happy with the way you are living your life or the way things are presently going?" Generally, after they have bonded with you they tend to tell you the truth to your questions. They say,

"No, I don't like the way my life has been." I then talk about how things happen for a reason and today you are here for a special purpose.

"Be it by your higher power or by chance alone, you are here with the opportunity to take the steps necessary to change your life and be satisfied and happy." I next reinforce the concept that most of us are unhappy and have all kinds of ways to change our lives for the better.

The second theory which I would like to discus is the person centered mixture. Foremost, I would like to state that I do not believe that this theory dominates the program completely, but it merely assists in your efforts towards winning the client's attitude over to his/her becoming an active participant of the program. Carl Rogers later discovered that confrontation was an active element necessary in his theory so as to assist the clients in change. I believe that using empathic confliction statements may actually be more therapeutic than conflict alone. I do not believe that I have ever attended a workshop which centered upon teaching empathic confrontation.

Most confrontationists tend to subscribe to the Frits Perls Method. As you can tell there is a proper place for this type of confrontation, especially in the area of drug and alcohol counseling. It is important that you remember that these clients have already been confronted by the courts, their families as well as everyone they have ever encountered, so it goes without saying that they are well aware of what they have done wrong.

The third method I would like to introduce to you is the Existential approach. The principle behind this approach is that you want the client to buy into the importance of his/her meaning and purpose in life and understand that their needs are currently being compromised through a mistaken meaning or misguided purpose. Consider for a moment that your client initially arrives at your class with the universal view that they are being punished. This is your opportunity to convince the client that change can alter his life making it more satisfying and happier. Seventy-five percent of the battle is accomplished by having them accept the program and that is primarily satisfied by way of the charisma and skills displayed by the instructor's interaction with the class.

In the past I have designed anger management programs for several other counselors. One time I did a program for a colleague of mine who wanted to teach the class since the child protection services would pay her to create and instruct the class. I was totally amazed that she knew very little about the subject at hand. I began with an outline filled with the usual basis concepts and submitted it to her. I even went as far as to include my video in the package which went into detail on the subject matter. My response was that she could not deal merely with an outline but rather she preferred for the information to be feed to her word by word. I in turn responded to the un-empathic confrontation that she would need to have some knowledge on how clients change and a firm grasp or understanding of the subject of anger. Unfortunately, she failed to pay for the program and we haven't spoken since. The moral learned here is that one should never mix business with friendship; you are bound to lose money, friends or both. This is an example of a potential counselor who had no business teaching anger management. There are other counselors that tend to be overly controlling or possibly stuck on their own issues involving rules as well.

My beliefs are that you as a counselor should accept the client as they are and empower them to desire to change by your program to make any necessary lifestyle and behavioral changes. It may very well be that sometimes your client may be content with where they are in life and don't really desire to change. However, you are still responsible for engaging them in the class by walking in front of them and asking their opinion on the various subject topics. Occasionally, you will experience clients who change while in the class environment or perhaps outside of the class while we as instructors don't always visualize the successful transformation taking place.

Let me relate an incident that I had with one of my clients. I had an individual we will refer to as George in one of my classes. George was on parole for the second time and the court had ordered him into a didactic anger group program. This was an open program that consisted only of eight attendance sessions in order to satisfy the requirements of the Texas Parole Board. George was a tall man of approximately six foot in height. He sported an abundant supply of various tattoos from his head to his toes. Upon his arrival the first day George was mad as hell that the parole board had forced him to attend the group sessions. He proceeded to walk up to me with his fierce body language revealing an,

"I don't want to be here and I am not gonna do shit in this group. You can tell my parole officer I said this, I don't really give a damn!"

George's attitude was not only confrontational but exceedingly scary as well. I knew it was vital that I showed no fear in my response and I attempted to be confrontationally empathic. I responded with,

"Its obvious you are angry about being placed into my class, however you will respect the others who do want to be here and benefit. So I expect you to sit down and be quiet, join in if you like, but you will complete your 8 sessions of mandatory program".

He immediately turned around and returned to his seat in the rear of the classroom. Not once did George interact with the class discussions but he did manage to complete all eight required sessions. During his exit interview he still did not have much to say as he was handed his certificate of completion. If the Parole board had an evaluation form involving participation and demonstrated learning, I regretfully would have had to assign George a big zero. He never once displayed any signs of interaction but merely listened. About six months later I received a Christmas card with a letter attached from George. The letter stated,

"Mr. Hayes,

Thank you for putting up with me in your class. Even though I did not interact and was obviously angry, I learned a lot and have changed my life for the better. I now go to church and assist troubled youths. I also have a spouse and children whom all seem to have benefited from my changes in life. Thank you as I wanted you to throw me out the first day. It shocked me when you didn't. This proved to me that you are a real person who cares as I have a long history of getting thrown out of treatment classes. Even though I didn't say much, I listened and many things you went over hit very close to my home issues. I even cried one night after class. I now see a counselor who is also assisting g me with my life. I just wanted you to know that your class and your patients inspired me to look deep inside of my self. Thank you for not allowing me to self sabotage at a point when I needed the most help. I am serious as I was even somewhat suicidal at that time. Now life is different and I have found what you call meaning and purpose.

God Bless,

George."

I almost fainted after reading this letter as I considered this to be one big break-through for myself. I was genuinely happy for George, but quickly realized that if I would have had to evaluate his class performance, I would have been dead wrong in my assessments.

"Buy me books and send me to school, but there is no lesson like experience."

The last I heard George was doing very well as I moved to another town and started a private practice. The lesson point here is don't judge the quality of your class by the performance or compliance of your students. Change often happens outside of your class session and away from the group.

Being an effective anger management instructor takes a lot of self awareness. It is vital that you as an instructor be in total touch with their own body language and effectively interact with the various clients. You can bet that your clients will quickly pick up on your body language. They can readily read when you are merely going through the motions in order to receive a paycheck. I truly believe this is one of those areas that lots of counselors fail to grasp and act on. You must become aware of your feelings. Ask yourself "Do you dread coming to class?" Listen to your thoughts, do they dislike working with generally confrontational, self absorbed people who tend to desire to rock the boat when smooth sailing?

Of course we are all human and have our bad days, however if this situation starts to become a cumbersome set of circumstances then I would highly suggest a long break to evaluate if this is really the kind of work you should be doing. Think of it as a situation where the client comes to us as is and it is our job to encourage them to become aware, think and challenge their thoughts, behaviors, reactive actions and their emotional impulses. We ourselves should set an example, and demonstrate to them that we are human and not only have problems ourselves but have to challenge our own identities the same as they do.

I myself have taught many anger management classes for free, this is how much I enjoy working with the angry client. One time I had to shorten my class by one day due to proposed building renovations. As I informed the clients about this upcoming situation I was pleasantly surprise to discover that they wanted to have that class anyway. In order to oblige them in their desires we met in the city park to include the material which I felt would be alright to skip over if necessary. This whole episode was incredible as we were talking here of court ordered clients and in view of this fact the complete class came to the park to get the whole program. I was certainly surprised.

Let's keep in mind that the human err I had involving George and that class which did not want to be short changed and thus met in the park were labeled by me. Unfortunately, this is a human thing which as instructors and counselors we must be continually aware of and try to see the good within everyone. These labels are powerful deterrents to progress and often times we will find that people allow themselves to live up to others labels and expectations.

We have all heard of the English teacher who labeled all her student as dumb. If you are not familiar with this tale I would like to repeat it here.

There was a young child with a learning disability that tended to receive bad grades and often acted out in class. The teacher was continuously negative in her interaction with the unruly child as she truly believed he was just a trouble maker. As the tale goes the teacher labeled the young child as dumb and the child eventually became aware of his teachers negative label projection of him. With this knowledge clearly in mind the child decided to test the system. The English teacher gave the class an assignment which involved writing a poem. The student upon receiving the assignment decided to copy a poem from 1960 that had previously won a Pulitzer Prize and turn the poem in as his own work.

He thought surely a Pulitzer Prize winning poem would receive a grade of an "A" on the project. The Teacher returned the assignments to the students after grading them and to his surprise he received a "D" as his grade. The student then decided he would challenge the grading system and accused it of being biased and unfair. To this he was punished for revealing he had copied the poem. The child was now accused of being a cheater. You can quickly gather and see that labels can be very powerful when projected by authority figures. Even the other teachers and the school principal will buy into the label's power. The student, although proving his point, was still treated like the label that was applied to him by his teacher.

In my opinion the student demonstrated an awareness of intelligence that should have been awarded. We can only hope that this particular teacher was embarrassed after she was confronted with grading a Pulitzer Prize winning poem with a high school grade of D. The idea here is that we as counselor must always perceive our clients as human. We have all erred and it is highly possible that perhaps one or two of these clients do not belong in an anger management class as they may have merely been labeled by the system. Treat them all with respect and dignity.

Chapter 2

As I think back to my early days when I was first requested to design and establish an anger management class there simply was not much available information involving the classes themselves. Since I was well trained and possessed experience in working with angry clients I naturally asked myself as to what were the important points which these angry people should obtain from a class of this nature? I proceeded to draw up an outline by initially identifying every major goal, listing the procedures on how to communicate the information and finally notating how to actively motivate the client to actually participate in the various sessions.

From my experience, I was aware that most of the currently available anger management workshops generally taught what anger was, how destructive its influence was to families and the person themselves and the legal aspects associated with physical violence. The problem that I discovered with most of these classes was that they failed to address the issue of becoming less angry. This I soon discovered was an open pattern within many of the workshops that I attended. Their downfall was that they simply failed to explain the inner workings of the subject in a pragmatic manner and never actually provided any interventions other than the usual recommendations of slowing down and counting to ten or for the angry person to merely walk away. If you were to attend one of the anger management workshops which were based upon the Ventalist Theory then you would be instructed to hit things with foam sticks or to yell and express openly those hostile thoughts which are frequently bottled up inside and to use those actions which would allow you to vent your anger in an appropriate way. This system may work for a few clients but the majority of my clients were already well aware of how to vent their anger. Let's face it that is exactly what got them into this situation to begin with, they vented their anger inappropriately.

I caution many potential instructors who subscribe to the Ventalist Theory to use caution as I am a firm believer in behavior tactics. If a person learns or becomes conditioned to strike objects such as pillows when they are feeling angry then perhaps during times when there are no pillows around possibly people would be an easy substitute. However, in the event that one of your clients informs you that this type of intervention system works successfully for them by all means do not challenge it. The key here is to be certain that they understand that those methods which work for some people may not necessarily be right for others. Point out to them that in this class we prefer to learn deescalating anger techniques which can be easily applied within any environment.

My critique concerning the Ventalist Theory is that it takes tremendous self control to actually work. As an example, I am a firm believer that by the use of fake sticks or using pillows as a weapon to strike other people we are just asking for trouble when the individual is confronted in the real world. In its place I would highly recommend replacing the act of hitting people with some sort of physical exercise such as running, weight lifting or strenuous work similar to splitting wood. These method are appropriate methods of venting ones anger without getting into trouble. These techniques are not always a readily available option in the real world environment. Let's suppose your angry at your boss for yelling at you what course of action would a Ventalist recommend? More then likely they would suggest that you leave the hostile situation and retreat to a safe location such as your car, roll up your car windows and just scream it all out.

Your boss is probably not eager for you to just leave a heated conversation, nor at possibly watching you make a total jerk out of yourself in the confines of your car. He is likely to notify security and may possibly start to question your mental health. My intervention of de-escalation and having a pre-behavioral reaction act previously prepared would allow you to defuse the situation with grace and dignity. To further illustrate my point suppose the boss is loudly yelling at you and shouting things like,

"I don't understand how someone can screw up so badly, this is important and what do you do? Nothing, what do you have to say for yourself?"

You may respond with, "I understand your anger and feel the same way. I'm getting right on the situation."

At this point you should attempt to leave unless you are still held captive by your boss. Your immediate response to your bosses venting should be....

(1) You are aware of his frustration and you completely agree that the results provided were inadequate.

(2) Assure your boss that you are on top of the situation and that you have identified the area that needs to be changed and that you will have a better outcome if he would permit you to get started now.

These actions impart your eagerness to attempt to use effective communications to deescalate the immediacy of the situation involving an angry boss who may be venting his or her frustration out on you. Give sufficient time for your boss to calm down while you attempt to eliminate the problem. Often times you will find many people that will allow a verbal anger abuse situation to motivate them to quit a very good job. Let's face reality, from time to time these occurrences are bound to happen at work and every worker at one time or other gets their fair share of being in the "pit". Of course it sucks, as you stand in front of your boss and take a whipping you naturally feel lonely, incompetent, angry and stressed out.

One technique that was useful to me when it was my turn in the pit was that I would ask myself

"How am I feeling right now and what am I thinking?"

The answer would usually be I am angry and feel like turning in my termination notice. I would then implant in my mind a cognitive de-escalation challenging thought such as "Give it two weeks and if I still feel the same way, then I need to go ahead and give my resignation." This technique has worked for me a thousand times for time does manage to change things and allows one to regain their focus. Usually after the two week period has passed one finds that someone else is then experiencing the so called "pit" adventure with the boss.

Starting an anger management program is easy if you know your theory and how it brings about changes within your clients. These are the very basic theories involved in counseling. They are known as the "Person Centered" by Rogers, the "Rational Emotive Behavioral theory" by Albert Ellis, the "Cognitive theory" by the cognitive camp such as Micalebom.

Other theories include Behaviorism which was discovered by Watson and ultimately made famous by Skinner. The principles set forth in "Social Learning Theorist" such as Lazarus, "Existential" by Frankle and May and finally "Gestalt" by Perls. These theories have evolved tremendously over the years and now incorporate many developmental issues and Nero-psychoactive chemicals. It is likely that today they may even be known by different names such as DBT or other newly named processes. Regardless of what they are now called each of them can be generally traced down to the basic theories mentioned above. The main feature is how they usually have the client implement the needed change.

Be actively aware of the environment for which you are implementing the program within as many environments tend to be full of controlling individuals contributing to a feeling of unhealthiness within the environment. One time I accepted a position as a clinical director at an in-patient adolescent agency. This agency was in great need of new directions and guidance. The boss that interviewed and hired me had been in her current position for over twenty years and ran the organization as she saw fit. When I was hired I was quickly informed of all the chaos in the organization and how she wanted me to step in and initiate necessary changes to make things operate smoothly.

I was highly motivated in this job. Not because it was my first supervisory position, but more so as it was my first time to be paid fairly for my labors. Upon my arrival I witnessed many unhealthy issues and methods used by the staff. Naturally as one would expect I was negatively met with tremendous resistance for any changes that I attempted to implement, after all this unhealthy system had been in operation now for years and no one desired to see it changed.

One of my first observations was that they allowed the staff to sit in on the group meetings and police the clients. In contrast, I was used to the counselor leading the group and simply guiding the natural group process to take effect. I experienced a client within the class and it was suggested I engage in a silence technique. Yes, you guessed it correctly the staff in attendance felt uncomfortable and continually interrupted the session as they put the client down concerning his past behavior. These completely inappropriate actions by the staff totally distracted the client from becoming aware of an effective therapeutic moment. When I attempted to remove the staff from the group I was met with unhealthy resistance from another co-worker who had the same power as the clinical director.

Of course my unhealthy boss sided with her on the subject of the staff being in group. I personally felt that the counselor should be the one who makes that call according to his particular group dynamic style. While some wanted to do the group with my suggested approach others desired various structural approaches as substitutes. In my opinion those who needed the staff in order to enforce the group rules tended to never achieve the desired flow involving the group process. It gave me an artificial feeling when I would monitor their group. The more I pushed the more I discovered that I was not the political favorite so I eventually had to compromise to a certain degree as that was a fact which simply was not going to change in the least at this point.

After getting to know the counselors I discovered that some could not even explain the process of change in a client. One even had this fantasy idea that they just magically change from merely talking with her. Unfortunately, as I attempted to make other changes I was once again met with sever opposition. At one point I spent an entire week composing a $100,000 prevention grant which I might add I was very familiar with as a result of my employment at Crossroads Council on Alcohol and Drug Abuse. Upon finishing the documentation I was confronted by my Supervisor who expressed that I had hurt my co-workers feelings by omitting her in the grant.

I responded that she was the education administrator and that I was sure that we could place her in the operation of the program. No sooner had I finished my statement then I was informed to go get with her and co-write the grant. Following the advice of my supervisor I went to her and she responded like a child who failed to get her way. After I sat her down and explained the grant and what was required of our agency she flatly rejected it and commented that it would never work with Native Americans. I was appalled at her remarks as my research clearly showed that it would in fact work with minorities as it was nothing more than a supportive educational intervention and prevention model.

As you may have guessed I was over ruled by a person who lacked the proper credentials and license to do any client treatment. Her response was merely that we just won't do this grant as it won't work. What made the situation more amazing and confusing is the fact that my supervisor sided with my non-treatment licensed coworker's gut opinion. As you can see I was facing great resistance not by the client's but rather by the staff and the administration despite what ever the research may have indicated. I soon became well aware that they really didn't want a clinical director to come in and change things for the better but rather they wanted someone who thought and did things the way they had done them for the last twenty years.

It did not take me long to realized that this environment wasn't healthy for me and soon I mustered up the courage to give my resignation. This occurred at a time that they were ready for me to leave as well as they were intentionally understaffing counselors with excessive hours. Even I was being utilized as a counselor on top of my assigned clinical supervision duties. I finally had a heart to heart talk with my supervisor who was a controlling type of individual and did not accept criticism well. As a result of our meeting we both came to the conclusion that this place was not a proper location for me. I gave my thirty day resignation and they willfully accepted it and informed me that the thirty days was not needed. I quickly pack up my belongings and left without further ado.

I apparently greatly upset my boss as I had to confront her for holding the program back through her micromanagement, triangulation, and encapsulated experience. It was extremely hard leaving the great pay behind but emotionally it was liberating. The reason I told this story is to instill a sense of urgency that you can't teach anger management if you don't have any knowledge of how a client changes. You should not teach anger management if you feel that this is not an area of your interest and you have merely been assigned to teach it for your company or in order to make extra money. These clients are good at reading unconscious body language and they will quickly eat up many counselors who may be in it for the wrong reasons.

When you decide to do this kind of work please above all keep in mind that the environment needed to achieve success is a safe client supported environment. In short, the client may become angry with a staff member or an established policy so the client must be afforded the opportunity to feel safe expressing the things which he chooses to become angry about. If the client does not feel safe enough to disclose his true feelings then most likely they will only go through the motions and recite what he feels the counselor wants to hear.

A true anger management instructor is neither guarded nor afraid to assist the client in dealing with his anger ventilation, thoughts and beliefs, or controlling behaviors of other clients. I believe a true assessment of your class is reflected in the body language expressed by the client's upon completion and interviewing.

Chapter 3

"What is needed in an Anger Management Class"

In establishing any anger management class we must initially know what the population will be in order to determine what exactly is needed. Classes tend to differ slightly according to whether the class is an Adolescent Class or whether it is an Adult Class. Since we are invoking two different populations, we would naturally involve very different interactions amongst the two different populations. Since I plan to discus Adolescent classes in a separate chapter, we can dwell entirely upon the Adult Class at this time.

Several questions remain foremost in mind when establishing such a class. Questions such as are the adult clients classes court ordered? Are they being required to undertake an anger management program as a result of a divorce? Are the intended purposes for taking the class to satisfy parole or probation requirements? Did the client have a conflict at work and are they now required to attend these classes? In order to provide the maximum benefit to your client you must know your intended population. It's important that you fully realize the general purpose of your attendance for your class.

Sometimes your client may be reserved and resistant to opportunities to share the reason that they are placed into your program. For this reason you will find the enrollee forms that are required to be completed can be of great benefit. Each client that is enrolled in the class should fill out a form and the form should be screened by the instructor.

If we existed in a perfect world we could survive with an individual face to face session to accomplish the appropriate screening and enrollment process. However, we do not. It would be a grave mistake to allow a divorcing couple to attend the same class at the same time. I have had this situation occur one time in my earlier days of anger management teaching and quickly became aware that the couples attention will not be on focused upon him or herself. Their attention would instead be placed upon the soon-to-be ex-spouse's reactions and behaviors. In addition, this process hampers the grounding of safe disclosure for each of the divorcing client's.

Such a mistake in placement would likely induce severe projection between the two and the resulting interaction involving blaming of each other would rob both of them of a valuable learning experience.

Knowing your clientele's main purpose for attendance, their gender and their cultural values is stressed as an important bit of knowledge when presenting the program. If you have a parent in the group as a result of losing their temper and committing physical child abuse this should be regarded as an important element that you should be aware of and certainly should be address in further discuss during the exit interview.

As a result of my experience I highly recommend two interview sessions with the most critical being the exit interview. The exit interview is a time when you can verbally assess the clients progress and make recommendations or necessary referrals. If you have unlimited resources at your disposal such as when conducting classes at a state institution then perhaps you may wish to purchase an anger inventory in order to present both pre and post interviews. This is a great asset if your are afforded this luxury but usually in most outpatient settings the associated costs represent a severe factor in the client's received services, therefore purchasing inventory's is usually not accomplished as part of the service.

I would simply love to obtain testing on all of my clients prior to counseling but due to financial restraints I can only send the ones that indicate a serious need for this service. I have had many successful counseling patients which have effectively benefited and improved their situations and their lives without ever have been tested before entering the program.

We have so far discuses having two individual interviews as the best policy to follow placing particular emphasis upon the exit interview. These interviews will aid you in knowing the cliental and their purpose for attending your Anger Management Program. In addition, we must understand the purpose of our class and the environments, attitudes or expectations to be expected of the class members. Remember, the more restrictive the environment the less probability that the client will open up and achieve full benefit of your class work.

Next we covered the need for forms in assisting our evaluations. It was stressed that these forms were extremely important and necessary for a solid class structure. In this book I have included the forms which I have used in my personal classes. Feel free to reproduce these forms and you may use them at your own risk. Make certain to check with your attorney to ensure the legality and appropriateness of each form you use. Don't bypass the administration or the party which is sending clients to you as we for they have a right to know what forms and data you are collecting. I would like to state here and now that each state is different in their record keeping requirements.

I view anger management classes as an educational class. These classes are not therapy in any way but rather they represent genuine educational facilities in nature. However they can have therapeutic value if applied properly. They are not therapy, psychotherapy or should they be considered counseling. Unfortunately, this is a huge mistake often committed by officials as they tend to perceive the incorrect structure of anger management classes.

One reasonable argument in favor of the class being considered an educational environment is that the DSM IV does not have any diagnosis of anger. Of course, you can readily find diagnosis which possess anger reactive behavior episodes as a primary condition of satisfying the diagnosis, however there is no diagnosis for being angry. DSM IV tends to recognize anxiety and depression as a mood disorder diagnosis.

Now that we have established a purpose within your organization and the cliental population has been properly identified for your anger management educational program a referral source is usually required in order to establish an anger management class. Believe it or not this type of client seldom volunteers for this educational opportunity. Having prepared an outline clearly stating the goals of the services offered and provided are a great asset when visiting with a judge or the county attorney. Keep in mind as you setup your class notes that there are education agencies such as schools or perhaps businesses which may utilize your class as a service to their students or employees. In such cases you will need a good referral source to stay in business. Never make the mistake of offering the class for free thinking the clients will return to you for additional counseling as I have seen other counselors do just this and ultimately ended up going out of business. From my previous experience this does occasionally happen but in a very slow pace of possibly one to three years later.

As mentioned above you should have all your forms reviewed by an attorney prior to the start of your anger management class. If you do not have an attorney to review your form here are some topics that I found especially important.

(1) A Pre-agreement to mediate any disputes arising from the attendee and the agreement for non-filing of civil suit against the instructor or his family. Both parties agree to adhere to the results of the mediation.

(2) Student gives their consent to attend and not to use the material as fact but rather to use the material with the understanding that it may or may not work for students.

(3) Consent to release information to referring party.

(4) To pay instructor fees of $500 a day if subpoena in any court proceeding whether that proceeding be of a criminal or civil nature due to student and instructors interaction and enrollment or denial of enrollment into the class.

(5) If the student violates the pre-mediation agreement and files civil suit then student agrees to pay instructors attorney fees, court costs, and all expenses occurred as result of said suit.

(6) Instructor is not responsible for any behavioral act committed by student after completion of class.

(7)   Student agrees that anger class is intended for educational purposes and not to be confused as therapy or treatment.

Understand I am not an attorney and can not give legal advice, nor am I claiming that my forms will meet your legal needs.

The above topics are merely a few of the legal issues that I have found to be important and should be adequately discussed with your attorney. A serious discussion with your legal representative concerning your class involvement and dealing with the associated liabilities with angry court ordered clients is absolutely necessary. A good attorney will find many more areas that should be taken into consideration with your independent class as well as protecting your legal standing.

After providing due consideration to all the information provided above you should be ready to begin your anger management class. I must reveal to you that my largest referral base came from county attorneys who make plea bargains with people who were charged with assault for the first time. This action tends to clear the courts of the misdemeanor first time offenders and serves the clients needs of proper awareness, education and consequence.

Chapter 4

Dealing with Adolescent Anger Management Class

Adolescents tend to display a vast difference in their developmental cognition and are often motivated differently then the adults. Many parents feel threatened when confronted by a rebelling teenager. I have witnessed many parent and child interactions which lead to the appearances in the juvenile court system. This group of clients are generally extremely challenging and the people themselves are naturally very rewarding to work with when instructing the applicable anger management classes.

Initially when dealing with these types of classes we must be adequately aware of the development model as seen within the adolescents. Erickson discusses that the moderator should attempt to form an identity stage by creating different role situations. This activity is usually referred to as "Identity Formation vs. Role Confusion". As we understand Erickson attempts here it becomes clear that he is attempting to establish a separation from the parent and in the process he performs different roles until the proper identity is established.

This population of clients is usually very motivated by their peers or by the thought of fitting in with the group or the imaginary audience. Interpreting these desires indicates that the parental influence is no longer as powerful over the thoughts of the adolescent as it previous was during their childhood years. At this stage of their life the adolescent is more motivated by peer interaction, peer values and acceptance by their peer groups rather then by any associates concerning their home life. With attitudes such as these the child's parents often become very agitated as they are aware that many of these role modeling actions displayed by their adolescent is not concurrent with the values they have tried to instill within their offspring. This type of action threatens the parent's perception of control as a parental role action. Therefore, prior to any adolescent anger management class taking place, I will meet personally with the parents in a group atmosphere for a thirty minute session in order to explain this particular developmental issue.

During this pre-meeting with the parents I attempt to do my best to assist them in understanding that some of the rebellion which they are experiencing is natural and healthy. In addition, I let the parents know that I can not force them to use these methods or any of the techniques that I explain within their daily lives. The point to be made here is that, I am merely going to present a series of tools useable by them to change their lives by the process of anger de-escalation however, it is ultimately up to them to take full advantage of them. Under no circumstances will I permit a parent to attend any of my adolescent anger management classes as that only tends to hamper the client's freedom to vent their frustrations, express concerns and issues as well as violating the factor of trust. I feel that these adolescents have enough issues with acceptance and it is already a challenge for them to speak out and participate is a session as it is without additional burdens being placed upon them.

It has been helpful to assure the parents that usually at some later time in the clients young adult lives, that they will generally return to the normal actions expected and complete acceptance of the values established by the parent's upbringing. This frequently provides them with some relief and hope for the future. Encouragement is shown when they realize that they are not the only parent who is experiencing a child who is acting out of context and getting into conflicts with others. I often explain to the parent the value of acceptance and consideration and that their adolescent has made a bad choice in acting out and that any parent can have a child who does the same things.

I like to use my own model as a single parent of two boys as an example. My first son never gets into any sort of trouble however, my second son even though he was brought up in a similar manner tends to have a greater need for attention. He has acted out many times which in turn caused me to have to attend those embarrassing teacher-parent conferences. You goal is to put the parents at rest and eliminate them blaming either themselves or their spouse. You should attempt to educate them of the need for separation between the parent and the adolescents in order for them to establish some sort of identity formation. During you sessions it is likely that you will find some that do not have the coping skills developed to do that without creating some sort of conflict or rebellion.

It is your responsibility to empower the parent to begin preparing for drastic changes within the family system. Stress should be placed upon the establishment of supportive change which is better than confliction change. Even though the adolescent may at this time display an attitude and act as if he or she does not require the parents support in all reality they actually do.

It is hoped that these messages will empower the parent with the concept that things can improve greatly if they would also change their expectations and beliefs. It is a known fact that any change made by one member in a family system can and will effect and change the system as a whole. I frequently recommend reading a book about parenting adolescents since the more parents that are aware of the needs of the adolescents then the more prepared they are for this stage of development.

Another issue which often presents dual effects upon adolescents is the constant changing of environmental expectations. Take for instance a parent who depends upon the teenager to baby sit a younger sibling. At this point the teen is expected to behave as an adult since you are empowering this adolescent with an adult responsibility. After all, you would expect and desire a responsible baby-sitter for your younger child.

As you can readily see you have bestowed upon this teenager a role usually reserved for adults. Now suppose this same adolescent later asks you if they can attend a concert which you strongly disapprove of. Chances are great that you will respond with "No". The adolescent is now changing roles of adaptation from that of a responsible adult trusted with the care of a younger child to that of a child who can not be trusted to perform responsibly. As you may quickly gather these contradictions can often cause a great deal of confusion and irritation to the adolescent. They frequently view this act as hypocritical parenting and displays gross inconsistencies.

This is one reason that the adolescent fails to listen to the parent. I am not sure that I would even listen to a parent which seems to always make decisions which address his or her particular needs. Don't get me wrong as I am not indicating that your adolescent can't baby sit but what I am stating is that a parent must use the same level of trust consistently when making decisions about the adolescent's growth. We as adults and parents should expect our adolescent to make mistakes in their decision making, especially in the decisions involving their own lives. This is exactly how many young people learn. We could refer to these as experiential moments and these serve as a great support for later learning experiences in their growth and development. Of particular interest is the idea that if the adolescent happens to make a mistake when they are babysitting their younger sibling, the parent appears more forgiving then they do if the situation concerns the teen's life itself. Perhaps this is probably the case that if the parents were to not forgo the situation they would simply be left without a future babysitter.

Schools are typical offenders in this regard as they will treat the adolescent as an adult in many situations while suddenly switching and treating them as children. This American inconsistency of treatment can be seen in many common daily activities. Let me provide you with one sample at this time. Our school's frequently have a student's parent write a sick letter to the school for a missed day however, many seniors are eighteen years old and are legally considered an adult. Regardless, these students are still required to get their parents to write an illness excuse for them before they may return to school.

Schools have also progressed from *In parentis* guidance to a more criminal justice model. Allow me to explain in further detail. *In parentis* guidance is a Latin word meaning to treat as a parental relationship in dealing with infractions. What this encounters is that if a teenager were to get into a fight then they would be punished with consequences similar to ones own child. However, the system is utilizing the courts in their efforts to deter negative behavior and now these same adolescents can be criminally charged with assault in the court systems. This may probably be necessary in some situations but I feel it has come to be much too relied upon by the school systems.

The schools tend to employ the school police as discipline integrationists. I personally feel that this violates the student's civil rights as they fail to understand when the school officer is honestly exhibiting sympathy and understanding with their assistance or if they are merely being interrogated for possible criminal charges or infractions without a parent or attorney present. The officer can switch purposes at his sole discretion.

The parents will usually back up the policeman's decision until such time as he does this to their child and gives them a citation for disorderly conduct. When the parent disagrees with the findings and they gather at court they find out that the police officer has obtained a recorded confession from their child without an adult or attorney present. It is unknown whether the adolescents may have confessed to the crime in order to protect others or merely to have the police drop the situation.

I know of a child who was questioned similarly by the school police about a morphed picture of a member of the opposite sex. He flatly denied doing it for about an hour and after seeing that the policeman wasn't going to accept the truth, he confessed to doing it. This child confused only to get the officer off his case and to protect his friend who admitted to me that he had been the perpetrator of the picture. Come to find out the police officer was emotionally biased as the picture which was morphed image of someone who happened to be a family member of his. So do not be fooled into thinking that an adolescent will not confess to doing something they didn't do as it does happen.

After I meet with the parents and respond to any of their concerns and questions, I next move on to the actual class. As I eye the class and make many mental notes, I see a lot of energy which is being used in a destructive manner by these young individuals. Jokingly, I often say that there seems to be a lot of young and up coming lawyers in these classes as they will quote many laws that they believe justified their actions. After listening to them all, I then challenge them to look at their interactions and ask themselves,

"Did you get what you wanted? Take a look at yourself and all that you had to endure, courts, parents, school and the police."

I next go on to say "If you are satisfied with the outcome then fine keep doing what you have been doing. Yes that's right, just keep on doing what you are doing and eventually you will wind up in a hospital, graveyard, jail or in treatment. That is because you have already ended up in an anger management class, the others are progression. See if you don't know the definition of insanity is doing something over and over and expecting a different outcome. Now that I have your attention, what if I could give you some tools that would get you some of those things that you really want?"

This starts to get their attention immediately and I then attempt to use empathy to win the adolescents over towards my way of thinking. I explain to them that they are currently in one of the hardest times of their life, the Transition! They are too young to be an adult but too old to be a child, they are stuck in the middle. I follow up with a talk about the light at the end of the tunnel and how when they become my age, they will long to move back in with their parents. At this point most of the adolescents in the class usually lighten up and begin to laugh.

I next move on to the motivational empowerment. I relate to them that if they were to start right now and show a dedicated effort, then they could achieve what ever they desire in their life. No matter what has happened in the past, they have the power to clear that slate and start over. There is nothing like the power one has in the "here and now".

If you were to think about what I said in the above paragraph you would see that I am using their need for power and control in order to assist them in changing their lives.

I used italic on the above statement as this is of utmost importance in working with adolescents. Use their strengths to empower and improve their lives. Never focus upon their weakness since I am sure that many in their lives have already pointed out their flaws. I then recant the information that covers anger management and how it applied to their lives in a modeling experience. By the time I reach the end of my material presentation I am discussing techniques with them. Once again I challenge them with the idea of "what would you say if I could teach you a way to change your communication methods in ways that would deescalate conflicts between you and your parents, or peers?"

It is highly likely that at this time I have them 100 percent into my way of thinking and so I venture into instructing them on effective communication skills that could offset future conflicts. To begin the discussion I start out with a true story centered around one of my personal conflicts with my father when I was 16 years of age. My father had arrived home from work and noticed that I had failed to mow the lawn. When he saw that I had not completed my chore he was outraged. It is possible that he had a bad day at work and this was merely the icing on the cake. All I know is he came and got me and was yelling loudly. I teach my sessions that at those moments we need to be aware of the emotion that our parent is exhibiting and what they are saying. My particular conversation went as follows,

"Joe, Damn it all I asked you to do was to mow the yard and you gave me your word that it would be finished by now! I work my butt off to give you a good home and you do this, now why the hell isn't the yard mowed!!!?"

Most of us fall into the human habit of making excuses and when I would try that technique, it would only escalate my father's reaction. Let's face it as an adult I now understand that when you expect something from someone and they don't come through with their promise but only provide you with a million excuses as to why they didn't accomplish the job it tends to only escalate ones anger. Since I am teaching a class on communication techniques aimed at deescalating anger I would then provide them an example of this type of action. They must:

> (a) First recognize his emotion, in this case anger.
>
> (b) Next they must hear what he is really saying. Sometimes this can takes practice as you must interpret the persons underlying expression - "what I hear him saying is he is mad that I didn't mow the lawn when I said I would so this leaves him unable to count on me when I say or commit to doing a task"
>
> (c) My reaction can not be one of making excuses or challenging my father when he is experiencing anger.
>
> (d) My reaction must communicate to him that I hear him and agree and fully understand him being angry. I will make it my priority to make the situation right. In a sense I am accepting the responsibility for what went wrong and

communicating that I will take action to make it a right.

By following the above recommendations my reaction to my fathers encounter would perhaps go something like this,

"It's my fault and I don't blame you for being angry. I will get on top of it now. Your right, let me go get started now"

I would then immediately exit from my angry father and follow through with the actions showing him that I care and have heard his complaint. Attempting to make it right has now become first priority. An angry person usually desires only to be heard and validated. After you have properly communicated and meet those needs above the angry person begins to deescalate on their own.

With that said I would now like to show you the other side of the coin. Here we show the reaction with excuses or with the "I don't care" attitude.

"Dad I was too tired from staying up late last night watching TV!"

Dad would have responded with

"I don't give a damn how tired you are when I tell you to mow the yard, you better mow the ******* yard!"

As you can readily see we are now caught up into a trap of passing the angry fiery metaphoric ball back in forth until one of us really gets burned. Believe it or not he who has the least amount of power will more than likely pay the consequence of getting burned. This is generally how most interactions escalate into verbal abuse or physical violence which neither side really desires.

There are often fathers or parents in general that possibly need to be in anger management as well. It is likely that they may even need some sort of counseling. If this happens to be your case, I would recommend a visit to your school counselor, probation officer, or preacher and getting them to invite the parent to a meeting to discuss possible family therapy. By doing so you are showing that you as a child are afraid of parent reaction and would like some help in the situation. As an adolescents these children are protected by laws from abuse and should be very careful not to cause anyone harm.

Now that you have instructed the adolescent with adequate communication skills that they can use with their family or peers, it is up to him or her to actually implement the necessary change. As a therapist my views are that parenting is effectively over after the age of 14. Of course, guidance is always warranted however my main goal is to encourage the adolescent to learn adaptive coping skills that will enable him or her to develop and mature with independence and dignity during the transition to a young adult. It may be difficult but parents can not expect to treat their adolescent like a child at the age of 17 and then automatically when they turn 18 he or she is expected to be an adult. If by chance the adolescent is so far out of their boundary's then be advised that there are places that can address his or her special needs.

To sum it all up, you are not dealing with machines, these are people with feelings the same as you and I. A helicopter mechanic fresh out of the army took a job position as a case manager for students at an "at-risk" special school. He ultimately sought consultation from me and one day he appeared to me extremely frustrated. He proceeded to explain how he had been working with one child in particular and had spent several hours on providing help for him. All his efforts were a failure in his eyes as the student continued to get into severe trouble with the law ultimately quitting school. He related to me that "It's not the same, when I work hard and long on a helicopter it worked. If I applied 90 pounds of pressure on a wrench, that is what I got back was a nut tightened to the 90 pounds. I work with a kid and go above and beyond and find it to be all for nothing".

Of course I came to his rescue and quickly pointed out change sometimes happens down the road or at another point in time. I explained how the client has to be ready to change and we as counselors have no power over that factor other than possible motivation through influence. No two children are alike. What works with one child may not work at all with another. They are all individuals and even the best of experts are occasionally outwitted by them. What matters is that you did the best you could when considering the heavily favoring odds of failure involving that segment of our population. What is important is taking care of yourself so that you are available and remain healthy for the ones who are ready to change. I then told him the Star Fish story.

Chapter5

The Cool Anger Model (Origins & Faulty Beliefs)

The Cool Anger Model originated as a result of my personal work involving court ordered criminal justice assigned adult substance abuse clients, rebellious "At-Risk" teenagers and parole clients. After a matter of four or five years of dedicated therapy with the above population, I noticed there were prominent thematic issues which tended to apply across the spectrum for my clients. In addition, I become aware of the same issues associated with angry clients during my many workshops that dealt with the subject. When I completed a particular workshop that was a certified state anger management program known as "RETHINK", I began to value the program greatly. It took an educational look at the vast developmental issues and directly applied family therapy techniques with its intervention program associated with the clients.

Of course there were also cognitive techniques involved but the program mainly addressed the family as a whole when treating the client's problems. The program eventually ran its course with the state agencies and was no longer funded. It was not longer after that I was requested by the director of Crossroads Council on Alcohol and Drug

Abuse to design a model for use by the courts. The county courts wanted such a program developed and thus we foreseen the birth of the Cool Anger Management Program.

This program emphasized empowering the client through their own awareness to seek a desire for change by way of a strong "Existential Theory" grounded base. I had discovered that after personally attending many workshops in the subject, I would leave them with the same pattern of thoughts. These workshops would address definitions and the origins of anger but they failed to make the information easily understandable. They also failed to provide much insight into the various techniques associated with anger de-escalation other than the usual breathing exercises, walking away or venting ones anger through other appropriate avenues. I truly felt that most of these programs missed the point involving the clients since most clients have no difficulty venting their anger and the majority of them do not have the awareness nor patients to simply walk away. It doesn't take a rocket scientist to realize that when they walk away their mind is still compounding thoughts of anger related reactions.

Yes, there is more to Anger Management than just walking away and on top of that most clients may not be able to merely walk away. Imagine getting angry in your probation officers cubical and just getting up and walking away or while as you are being questioned by law enforcement officers you try to leave. I think you can see my point here.

The other programs that are created for anger management, I feel do not properly address the bottom underlying issues. With these thoughts in mind I decided to design a program which was easily understood and pragmatic towards applying it to daily life. The model focuses upon living a meaningful and purposeful life, developing a full understanding of what anger is and the effects that it has upon us, as well as the empowerment which we actually process and can use to efficiently bring about behavioral change in our reactions.

I always begin my session with an empathic group listening where the client can express their interpretation of why they are in attendance. I then reinforce their outspoken honesty which the question has brought out, such as "I am only here because I am ordered by the courts".

I am attempting at this point to form a "Gestalt" relationship with group and in particular the clients. Remember back to when we discussed the various theories; Gestalt's counseling relationship was formed by an interaction vs. relationship and not a warm and caring atmosphere as found with Rogerian. An exceptionally good book to read concerning this issue is entitled "In and Out of the Garbage Pail" by Perl. I am not saying that you should be as confrontational as Perl for that is more his personality then anything else. Confrontation is great but must be applied with the right timing and at the proper moment.

The time that a client enters the "here and now" is more therapeutic for accepting confrontational awareness as it tends to challenge his beliefs or behavior. This is the difference between a average instructor and a good instructor who grabs the client for the moment and maintains his attention immediately. You will find that at the beginning of your class you have a room full of angry clients who feel like they are being punished for their actions. I try to challenge them through empathy, getting them to open up and perhaps change their life and benefit through a result of this priceless change.

I next use the "Adlerian" technique known as "the magic wand" and request that each member consider the possibility that if they could change one item in their life what would it be? I further emphasis how great it would be if that change could result from attending today's class. This tends to get the clients thinking on the terms of no longer being a victim but rather to that of being a benefactor. In your class you should try this technique for yourself and see if you get several of the group members to buy into it. If so then you can reasonably expect the others to slowly join the band wagon.

The above procedure is based in part by the social psychology theory as proven by the Ash studies of group conformity. I have completed my experiment involving this theory and have discovered it to be a very important variable in persuasion. If you can accomplish this then you have made progress. You need not worry as many of the instructor qualities will eventually come with experience.

Results will not be the same each and every time and you may not witness success on a continual basis. You are not even expected to master all of these points from reading this manual. I would suggest that you also read a good group theory book written by Yalom or Corey & Corey. They go in depth into a major discussion of group dynamics and the related processes in more detail then what I do here. You need not find the most recent edition of these books as those readily available in a public library would serve your purposes just as well.

The most important trait that can be found in a good instructor or counselor is the ability to trust the group process to work as it should. This act may be difficult for many inexperienced instructors as they are unaware of their insecurity for needing to control the group. Believe me the natural process is much more powerful in effecting growth and developing awareness in clients. So I would highly recommend that you place trust and faith in the dynamics of the group evolution process.

An important point to remember is that you are facilitating the group and it is your expertise that is needed in order to keep monitoring the clients and to keep group members from harm. I have found that at times I have had to physically protect clients who tended to become scapegoats or those clients who were more assertive and had many unresolved issues. These problems were frequently projected onto vulnerable clients. Your primary duty is to facilitate the group into allowing the natural process to run its course and to do no harm to the various clients. As such in the event that you see there is a particular client being constantly picked on it is your duty to intervene and redirect that group member into a moment of self observation. In this way you can confront and move the group along towards final completion.

I prefer the Didactic model of group as it allows me to go over topics and issues and spot the directed energy of the group process itself. I follow it and even reinforce important statements through my body language and techniques. As an example suppose a group member outwardly states that "Change is scary". At this point I would stop and request that they repeat their statement again while stating the following.

"Change is Scary. That is right change is scary and life is full of scary challenging changes. So what changes have been scary that each one of you have encountered and succeeded in conquering?"

This technique is used to impress upon the client and make them aware that he or she has been challenged with many scary changes which may have occurred without any physical damage or harm.

I then address various faulty beliefs as well as the belief system itself with the group. I like to share a definition of a simple belief system with the members of the group. Although the Cool Anger's definition is also a belief system it is nothing more than the manner in which we talk to ourselves. These options can be conscious or unconscious in nature. There is actually a difference between a lie and the act of being in denial. I would show the class videos and instruct them to watch them as I do a precognitive set in order to demonstrate the difference between conscious and unconsciousness actions.

There are some belief systems which have common elements with anger management programs. The number one belief system states that "Life is always fair." This is the number one belief system that has been the bases of many perceived causes of people allowing themselves to react with angry behavior responses. Another faulty belief is "We always get a second chance to do something right". This belief is sometimes reinforced by our society while in other situations it is invalidated. For this reason if no other I often inform my clients that sometimes certain behaviors may be permanent and there is no guarantee that we will get a second chance to make the situation right. I further advise them that it is their responsibility to use all the tools available to make the best decision that they can at that moment.

In the video I discuss the many physical altercations which start out as a common fight but quickly escalated in one where a weapon is pulled, permanently injuring or killing another person. After all is done it is these people who wish that they could turn back time and redo the whole situation. Believe me, most of them never intended to cause such harm. One example that comes to mind is a drunk driver who crashes into an innocent person causing irreplaceable harm. That person's ultimate moment of decision was that point in time when he or she placed the keys into the ignition while they were intoxicated. That was the moment when they forfeited their power of choice. Now after the fact, I am certain they are remorseful although I expect that most still feel they deserve a second chance.

This is a very sad situation as the reality of it all is that the harmed individual doesn't get a second chance. They are either severely wounded for life or no longer living. The third common faulty belief is "That everyone is going to like and accept me". I know your mother may have continually told you this during your upbringing but it is completely untrue.

There are personality conflicts which actively create difficulty in interaction with others. There are many people who have excess baggage and an assortment of unfinished business which is likely to be projected as the results from what others have done to them. As luck would often have it there may be something about you which tends to trigger these projections within the person. There are even environments which could conflict with your personality. I would venture to state that the more adaptable one is towards multiple environments, the more mentally and socially healthy their behaviors will be which they exhibit. Another recommendation for a good book which covers this issue in detail is entitled "Emotional Intelligence". An example from the book is a room full of doctors who are wanting a solution to a scientific issue and you may very well have the best researched pragmatic available.

If this group of professionals were to accept your idea strictly on the contingency of how well it is presented to the group you would likely do better if previous encounters had not already clouded the doctor's judgment about you. If this were you then you would have to graciously present your idea in a manner that would open up your new perceptions for the group to consider.

I have seen many quality ideas totally shot down in meetings before they were given adequate consideration. It is my contention that prior ideas about the presenting people may have already been formulated. What this amounts to is the fact that you are always selling yourself and not your products or work when it comes to employment, school or even in relationships. You can find many more faulty beliefs that you may wish to later add to your program. I have only a few at this time of which I felt were necessary to properly learn anger management. These three beliefs represent the most commonly encountered issues in the client's life.

In the next chapter I would like to show you how you can teach your clients to make positive changes. Always try to keep it as simple as you can for there are millions of theories involving change. I will talk about three motivators of change, which are Frustration, Mental Healthiness and the Existential event or better known as Acts of God. I shall also include how to change in the next chapter.

Chapter 6

Life changes from a counselors view

The process of change in a person is subjective and interpreted differently according to thee specific theories which one may follow. Year long arguments over Nature vs. Nurture still plague today's sciences. Throughout my career I have experienced an abundance of evidence concerning both traits which affects many clients' ability to process change. As would be expected, each client has a tendency to exhibit unique strengths and associated weaknesses. There simply is no one size fits all program that will apply to all clients at all times just as there is no wonder medication which will cure mental illness. Although the medicines' of today have undergone tremendous advanced they still only treat the symptoms without offering an effective cure for the illness.

This is exactly what makes weight loss change so unique, that is the changes which occur on the many different levels. The vast number of environmental systems where change must be experienced include the belief system, motivational system, reward system behavioral system, social system, family unit system and the physiological system. Even though changes in weight loss affect multiple systems; it all begins with one's own awareness.

Awareness is the first factor that we find necessary for free will change to occur within an individual. Without awareness we can have no free change at all. I have taken the liberty of identifying three factors which motivate a person to seek a desired change. These catalyst factors are frustration, comfort and Existential Events. They are explained in the following paragraphs:

(1)　Frustration - Clients become very sick and tired of living their lifestyle in the manner that they have been living; through various internal drives of frustration they often seek a major life change. This highlights my theory that the clients needs may not be properly met in their daily life. They tend to be going through the motions of their life either in a state of chaos or through a series of drastic dissatisfaction. Sometimes they may even experience a fear of change due to their self imposed comfort zone. They may likely become aware of self inflicted pent up feelings of frustration that surfaces which results in them seeking change by way of a fueled motivational driven purpose for seeking new meaning in their lives.

(2)   Mental Healthiness - The client seems motivated with a healthiness towards change. The client is actually living their meaning and purpose, but has the awareness to continue to grow and develop the healthiness of the internal self. These changes are necessary to continue living as we know full well that the alternative would be physiological cessation of change or commonly referred to as death. The mental self tends to change through a process of growth and development which is what I perceive as developing spirituality. These people as a result are in tune with ones meaning and purpose and nurture a continued self awareness relating to meaningful growth involving relationship to self, others and the universe.

(3)   An Existential Event/Act of God - This is an uncontrollable catalyst that can be identified as a powerful euphoric event in ones life which affects his or her meaning and purpose. Severql applications of this theory would be a near death experience, death of a loved one or a spiritual awakening. These influences represent a powerful impact upon a person

to change his or her ways and are samples of the Existential Event.

I often incorporate a formula for Free Will change which has been influenced by multiple theories. The formula contains the following critical steps:

(1) Awareness - One must initially become aware that a problem does in fact exist and then they must accept the idea that he/she has the responsibility to alter themselves in relation to the problem. Usually many folks find a trap is sprung when they believe they are in control of the situation. This concept haunts many people in addressing their problems and resolving their issues. Their error in thinking centers upon the idea that their behavior controls the situation.

Many of my clients end up having to attend Anger Management Class due to their behavior which results from reacting in response to this faulty internal belief. They may end up violating a law in their pursuit of a partner who perhaps no longer wishes to be their partner. I have often asked many of my clients

"What magical process were you thinking? Did your thinking go If I harass him or her long enough, then they will eventually come to their senses and say You were right, I love you and should of never left.

This error in thinking is easily compared to that person who believes that they can just walk out into a pouring rain storm and command the rain to stop. The logical thinking would be to use an adjustment reaction of opening an umbrella. My point here is that one cannot control situations that have happened or occurred to other people. You do however, have control over yourself and your perception and are afforded the opportunity to adjustment your reaction according to the situation.

(2) Insight/Direction - The client must have the ability to know what he wants to change. Most of the clients that I have dealt with inform me that they don't want to feel bad or depressed. I openly confront them with the concept that I can not help them with that which they don't really want. At this point I have not identified what they actually do want. I accomplish this task through many

techniques. As an example, my response would have been the question of

"What would you life be like if you were happy?"

This type of logic assists the client in identifying the parts of his life that he could change if he so desired to achieve happiness. This develops goals with a sense of direction for the client to pursue. The client must identify and know what direction is necessary to facilitate his desired change.

(3) Planning - Once the client identifies what he or she wants to accomplish then they can gather all the necessary information needed to form a plan for change. Although plans don't always work; the mere act of the client experiencing a feeling of independence through self empowerment and attempting to resolve their own issues could ready result in a positive therapeutic growth. Clients must learn to accept their failures as an inspiration to further pursue solutions that may possibly work and to not simply give up. This process strengthens the client's evaluation and coping skills since several attempts that result in no successful solution may force the client to reevaluate his or her goals.

Take for instances a forty year old out of work actor who after a number of years experiencing rejections for a vast quantity of major movie parts is finally forced to accept the idea that acting may be only a hobby and not their profession. The old saying that "if one or two people call you an elephant you should not worry however if numerous people consistently refer to you as an elephant then it may be time to buy some peanuts." The client should design a plan which utilizes their strengths and hope that the strengths make up for any weaknesses.

(4) Motivation - Motivation is similar to washing ones hands. You should do it daily until it becomes a natural habit. Motivation consists of two catalysts: Internal vs. External. When I worked at an In-Patient treatment center, I often noticed a lot of the developmentally delayed children would not always groom their hair. To remedy the situation I extrinsically started rewarding them for combing their hair. When using the shaping model such as this it will requires a gradual backing off of the reward to be considered successful. This process enables the external reward to develop into an internal reward. The ultimate goal is for the child to desire grooming their hair because it makes them

look good and they desire to look appeasing and well groomed, not because they receive a reward for doing so. External is a stronger reward in the short term race while internal remains stronger for the long term marathon. Lifestyle changes through weight loss reveals a similar pattern. One would need to make a true lifestyle intrinsic eating behavioral change to view their success.

Success stems in a positive correlation of a well balanced combination of the clients' motivation, awareness, willingness, meaning and purpose, direction and readiness to change. The above information may be used as is or it can even be modified for each client's specific needs. Remember, success isn't always the trait we are hoping will improve when we are doing the measuring. Sometimes success comes in other forms and as time wears on we become aware of it. This old saying pretty well sums this up "Thank God for unanswered prayers".

Change is scary to most people whether they admit it or not. These clients that are in your anger management class often are defensive and don't feel that they need to change. They frequently blame others for their problems and tend to shed their responsibility for the resulting conflict.

Your job as an instructor or counselor should be to teach anger management as a challenge to the client through the use of their own logic. As a result they are becoming aware of the life benefits from actually applying different ideas and changing themselves. Let's be real here it was their ideas, beliefs and behavior all rolled into one that got them originally placed into an anger management program. Maybe a little change in perception and reaction may benefit the client's quality of life. It represents a more powerful impression if the client is allowed to reinforce the concept that he needs life improvement and is actively motivated to assist himself in this goal. This process of change is broken down much simpler within the DVD and is merely elaborated here for the instructor's benefit.

Chapter 7

Happiness = True Meaning and Purpose

The Cool Angers Anger Management Programs main goal is to assist its clients in seeking a content and happy existence by living a meaningful and purposeful life. This factor is of the highest importance in achieving a successful lifestyle change. As mentioned earlier, people are motivated to change in three diverse ways - frustration, health, and existential happenings.

These areas are what cause so much anger, hurt and pain in a divorce. In a divorce, there is usually one person wants it while the other does not. Typically one of the persons involved in a divorce began the mental distancing process prior to the actual documentation of the divorce. At this point this person is the one who files for the divorce leaving the other person devastated.

Suppose for the sake of argument it is the man who did not desire a divorce. The man built his whole life's meaning and purpose around being married to his spouse. He made both many life and financial decisions based upon being together with that person. The sad part is that she has grown towards a different direction and no longer desires to be married. This action shatters the man's ideal of life and he feels as if he has been living an illusion or a lie. All of a sudden he is left alone and has to pick up the pieces of what he calls his life.

Once he finds and gets his needs met he is likely to rebound. At this point in his life he attempts to replace his spouse with perhaps another available female. This is his attempt to hang on to his old meaning and purpose for living. After a period of time the man begins to approach his reality and begins to see the person as someone other then who he thought she was. This is a typical sample of projection. Finally he leaves her because he realizes he was not in love with her to begin with. He finds it difficult to even contemplate the thought that he had previously considered and talked about marriage between them. He had previously been unconsciously driven to obtain a specific meaning and purpose to his life and then upon acceptance of this concept he sees that his happiness can only come through his pursuit of true meaning and purpose within his life.

People who live following a mistaken meaning are merely going through the motions of life. Their actions have become habit not an act of living. They may go to work on a daily basis or they may eat some cookies, perhaps watch Jay Leno late into the evening and finally arise the following day to repeat the same procedure once again. A meaning involving life can be multiple in nature. It is likely that you can find people that have totally different meanings associated with their life. I define a meaning as an identity coupled with a sense of belonging.

People will get their meaning met by the process of work, by companionship within their church, through a family centered structure or by their use of any other entities. An interesting comparison is changing your life through the process of weight loss as this will also affect your intended meaning and purpose in life. Many people who lose their excess weight finally realize that they were just going through the various motions of their life. Their important needs for stable identity and the feeling of belonging were not being truly met.

The purpose in life is the drive which keeps us going when the times become rough. My meaning in life is that I am a father, counselor, son, etc. while my purpose is to adequately raise my children and assist people in bringing about life changes. Within society you will find there are different multiple meanings as well as different, multiple purposes. Finding ones true meaning is similar to engaging in the pursuit of happiness. If you are not enjoying life then look at the area that seems to be keeping you from obtaining your true meaning and purpose.

Life is like a video game

Any gamer can tell you that there are lots of different games on the market created to meet a variety of different peoples' needs. Once you have found the game you like you only need to put a quarter in and start playing it. You quickly become excited by the behaviors of moving a lever or hitting various buttons. If I were to walk behind the machine and yank the plug from the wall you would still be able to move the lever and push the buttons however this would only be considered going through the motions. The problem with this is that there would no longer be any satisfaction in playing the game. By the mere act of pulling the plug from the wall I took away all meaning and purpose behind your behavior of moving the lever or pushing the buttons. Life is very similar in that respect since you may be just going through the motions and only moving levers or pushing buttons. In such case you are not likely to be happy.

Many people establish various claims that certain aspects of their life are important for their happiness however they tend to devote very little of their time to the completion of these values. Client after client will boldly claim that their children or their family are the most important items within their life and contribute greatly towards making them happy. I generally have them analysis the amount of time which they spend with their children in a seven day period. Talk about defensive attitudes. You will find that most people are snapped into reality when they become aware that they spend more time on their computer then they do interacting with their family and children.

I have even heard the argument that they spend quality time with their family and children so that is what really counts. I always challenge that type of logic with the comment that if quality time was food and I gave you just a small amount of the highest quality food once a week, I would bet you would still starve to death. So that argument as far as I am concerned is nothing less then an excuse. I reiterate to them that they would do well to remember that there will come a day later in their life when they will wish they had truly spent more quantity time with their family. This time usually arrives when the children are grown up for then they will contact you only for quality time. You can rest assured that they will place many things in front of family life and interaction the same way that you had taught them to do by your modeling behavior. A good movie which relates this theme well is Adam Sandler's "Click".

You are apt to discover other factors which may be biological and can come into play to aid you in achieving your happiness as well. That is the primary reason that doctors prescribe antidepressants and other medications. People can frequently have a hormonal imbalance or possibly sugar diabetes, all of which can cause mood disturbances. Be sure as a counselor that you rule out all medical causes and you should inform your client that if they continually try and try but still are not able to achieve a happy life then perhaps a medical checkup would be warranted. Even though some instructors often feel that depression is nothing more than anger which is directed inward at ones self there still may be a medical necessity that which is being over looked.

Chapter 8

What is Anger?

The cool anger management theory views anger as a learned responsive reaction which a person has learned to use when attempting to control his immediate environment or perhaps another person. In other words, it is a secondary emotion if one was to consider it an emotion at all. This learned response tends to be partially unconscious in nature. There is some awareness of the behavior reaction however the way it occurs is systematic in nature. I usually provide the clients with an outlined model of anger and proceed at that point to explain it in further detail.

First, let me state that there is a stimulus from the clients environment or some sort of trigger which affects the person. As an example suppose that an unknown male at your favorite bar makes a flirtatious comment to your girlfriend. You naturally perceive the actions as disrespectful since they were accomplished in your presence.

The clients personal inner voice may immediately kick in with statements such as, "Who the hell does he think he is?", "No, he didn't just disrespect me in front of my lady" or "He must be wanting an ass whooping today" These are merely examples of the inner voice that could triggers the clients learned anger reaction.

In the simple world this trigger would be identified as a person who is disrespecting you and would initiate one of two emotions. The stimulus will kick in one of the following:

The number one emotion that the client may experience is Fear. It could very well be argued that fear is the primary emotion found under anger however I generally include "hurt" as another emotion simply because it assists the general population in understanding where the anger originates from within us. Breaking down fear is an act of viewing the fear as an range of anxiety. This stems all the way from a small range of anxiety for being late for an appointment or a class to knowing there are possibly three thugs waiting for you outside with baseball bats. Both scenarios tend to promote anxiety but to totally opposite extremes.

The other emotion I would like to discuss causes the same reaction with ones self inner voice and functions the same way. As you may recall the inner voice is our perceived belief system that we perceive as reality. It is easy to see that one measure of occurrence is the stimulation necessary for one of the primary emotions of anger.

Diagram A.

ANGER MODEL

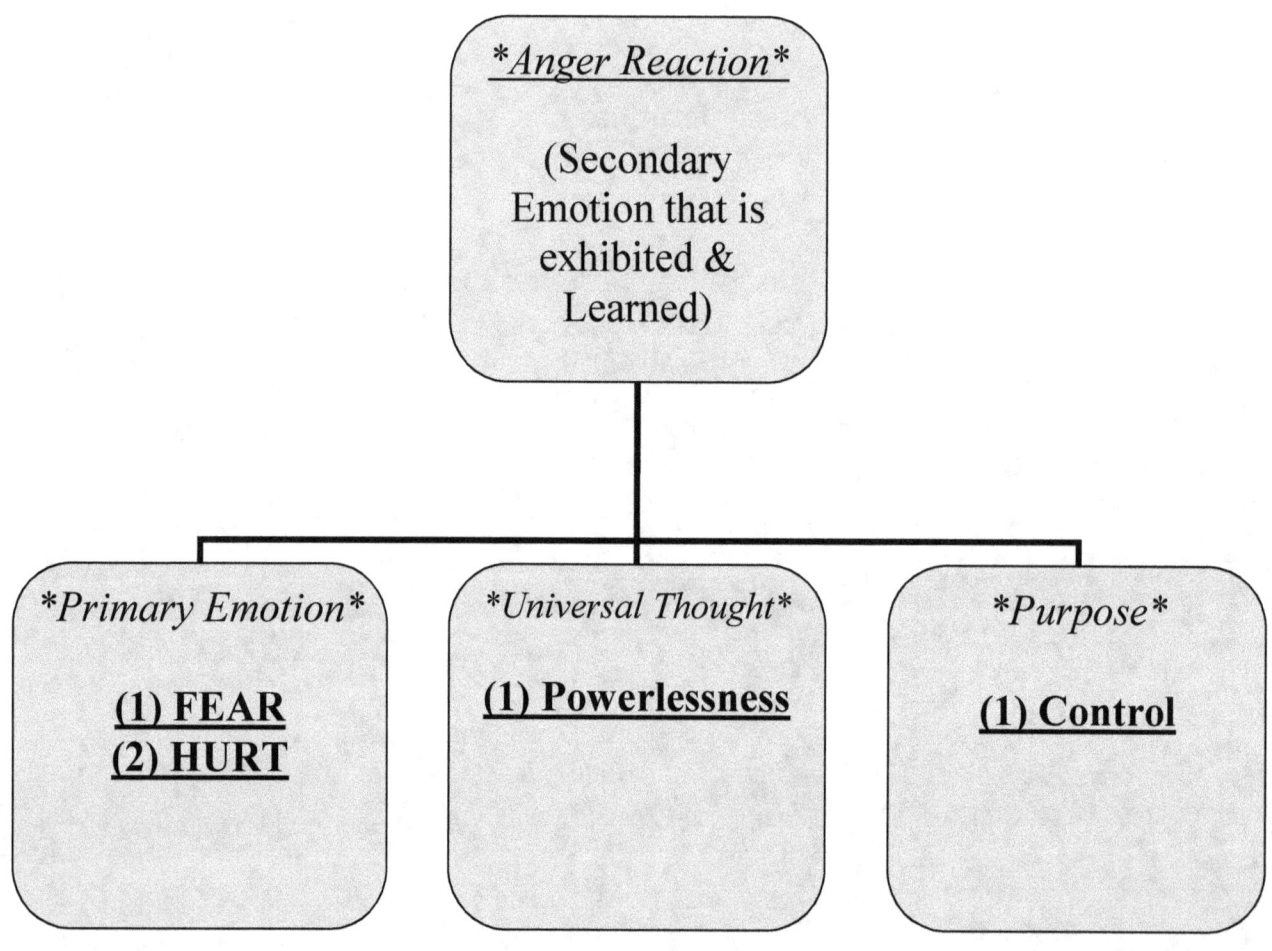

Anger Reaction

(Secondary Emotion that is exhibited & Learned)

Primary Emotion

(1) FEAR
(2) HURT

Universal Thought

(1) Powerlessness

Purpose

(1) Control

When one is well aware that he has experienced a stimulus from the environment and this reaction has stimulated one of his two primary feelings either fear or hurt then another cycle is about to occur simultaneous. This other cycle is what separates us from the animals and is collectively known as cognition.

The client may be feeling that he is powerless over a specific situation or person and this only tends to fuel the anger response he is feeling. Therefore the client views it for the purpose of any underlying behavioral anger reaction they must establish a sense of control for either the situation, a person or a group of people. The sad fact of this situation is that usually the more anger behavioral reaction that the client has exhibited the less control the individual actually tends to acquires. They often permit the aggression held inside to break loose and escape while another party actually steps in to take charge of the person or situation.

Although the individual has been rewarded throughout their life for exhibiting aggressive angered behavior due to the fact that by doing so they often times tend to get his or her way. In some environments that may have worked successfully for them but in a civilized environment it is doomed to failure. An example is the controlling husband who dictates to his spouse on everything that she undertakes. The wife initially may actually like that he is taking care of all her every needs however within time people often grow and mature. At this point the wife may desire more personal independence. As would be expected this desire threatens the husbands sense off control.

This *stimulates the primary emotion fear and universal thought of powerlessness.*

The husband is now bound to increase the anger reaction behavior until

(a) He gets what he wants,

(b) He reacts to a point that he has to be shut down by authorities or figure of power over him or

(c) He realizes this form of manipulation will no longer work in obtaining his desired results so there for he will implement other forms of manipulation.

As a person grows they tend to change perceptions and his wife was no exception. She modified her perception of her controlling husband' behavior until she finally got feed up or no longer cared. This type of conditioning is similar to that employed to teach helpless animals tricks as they are shocked on a continuous basis. At one point the animal may end up just giving up as they become aware of the situation. They perceive that regardless of what they do they will be shocked anyway. The same is true of the husband and wife. The husbands controlling anger behaviors tend to lose its fear inducing effect upon his spouse with a result that she becomes immune to the control.

What we have covered here is the Cool Anger Model that defines Anger. By developing the insight into why the various stimuli is stimulating our fear, hurt and powerlessness thoughts we can assist our clients in learning to better cope with developed skills necessary to deal with the individuals need for control. Usually we find an abundance of insecurities underlying the excessive need for control. Don't get me wrong, with certain issues it is healthy to have a positive control, such as when one must control their finances or career path. However the main point of trouble starts when we attempt to control another person or group of people.

The Anger reaction can often be used as a motivator. This technique has been successfully employed by the military as well as by various sports teams. If a person is capable of harnessing the energy which they put into being angry and they set a definable goal to accomplish then that would be a healthy use of angered response.

Allow me to provide you with a valid Life example. I quite school in the 11th grade. After two years of experiencing the resulting consequences of my decision, I got the thought of going back to school and finishing my education. I was completely shocked by my friends attitudes and even one counselor.

A girlfriend of mine told me "Joey Hayes you will never finish school, you are one of us flunkies." Needless to say that comment ate at my very soul. I immediately registered in school only to be confronted by a school counselor who commented "Joey Hayes, you won't ever graduate, why are you wasting everyone's time? You belong back in the streets where you came from." These people attempted to deflate my balloon.

It is sad that we never really receive the support that would accurately benefit us, but we sometimes get just enough to fill our needs. What I needed at that time was a challenge to prove to those people who had labeled me as a loser that I can make a valid difference in my life. I relied upon self belief and did not allow them to influence me in any way what so ever. That in my opinion would have been the ultimate sin. It is bad enough that other people put you down, but don't give them the satisfaction of you yourself buying into their labels.

In the next chapter I shall conclude my program with letting go and forgiving. I will mention how to shed those negative labels which people often attach to each of us.

Chapter 9

Letting Go Forgiving and shedding the Label

Empowerment comes when the client or student identifies and ultimately acknowledges that he has previously held onto some faulty beliefs in their past. The individual is now ready to let go of their past and to live once again. You can see these actions occurring at the time that you note the client challenging himself as an external change is the desired effect that you are seeking in the person. This same change is similar to the one that I would like my clients to understand in the area of parenting.

I firmly believe that they desire their children to behave as a result of the motivation involving their inner values and beliefs and not just to avoid punishment or threat of pain. Since we can readily find many clients who may previously have been labeled by others holding positions of authority they have learned to accept the idea that their inner beliefs about their self are what is important and not merely what others may project. Of utmost importance is the concept that the client must learn to forgive both themselves and others.

The process of letting go is actually one of the most difficult issues that can be presented to the client. The letting go process often tends to exhibit the same grief as was pointed out in Kubler Ross's stages of death. These stages are denial, anger, bargaining, depression and finally acceptance. Upon acceptance of these aspects of our life is where one begins to grow emotionally. This is the point in time where he has developed the power to alter his life through his own interventions.

An old saying which I have found to be especially true is the one which states "that one needs to live his life as if tomorrow is his last day to live." What this means is simply that if you were on your death bed would the issue which generated such anger in you be of any significance? I hope you can see where I am coming from with this statement? Letting go is like lifting a monkey off of ones back.

Forgiving is a powerful force as it assists us in living for the moment. Forgiving is the process of letting go and moving on with your life. A lot of people mistakenly think that we must forget in order to forgive but this is not the case. If that were true then we would merely be setting ourselves up for further harm. Even if we are able to forgive ourselves it is important that we never forget how we harmed ourselves. An example of this concept is that of a thief who successfully turns his life around after being placed in jailed. In this case the thief must forgive himself for his actions however he must always remember where his actions had previously taken him. These are considered Logical Consequences of the person's actions. The person would not want to repeat an older type of error involving his decision making results. Forgiving is a process which allows oneself to live in the here and now by letting go of the past.

At this point in the class you should be ready to teach an anger management class. I have included many of my forms, outlines, and videos in an effort to assist you in conducting the Cool Anger program. Please, by all means seek further knowledge and tweak the program to satisfy your needs. Remember you as the owner are responsible for ensuring all compliances and proper completion of the necessary forms. You will want to continue with your own education in the area of Anger Management. Keep clearly in mind that all this material is copyrighted and may not be reproduced in any color or fashion without the written consent of Joseph D. Hayes.

The original owner of this program may reproduce the forms and make changes as necessary to them in order to satisfy their need as long as they are the purchaser.

FORMS WILL FOLLOW

Cool Anger Management Program Agreement

Company or therapist name _____

Phone _____

This is a binding contract between the anger management teacher and the student and is meant to be interpreted as such. The student understands that this is an educational class and that is not to be considered treatment in any form or fashion. is the student's sole responsibility to check with the courts or referring party to make sure that this class will work for the purpose in which he is attending including legal ,civil, etc.. I will furnish a document after completion that state you have completed the course. If lost there will be a $15 replacement fee. Here are the other agreements that must be honored in order to attend class:

Instructor can remove any student from class without refund due to conduct or disruptions interpreted by the instructor.

If instructor is subpoenaed then the student who attended class takes responsibility to the instructor and pays fees plus expenses of cooperating with the subpoena (Criminal or Civil)

The Instructor charges $300 a day for any testimony with the payment of a $1000 deposit to be paid within three days of instructor receiving notice from any litigating party. (The $1000 will be used to draw fees and expenses from, the remainder will be refunded to the student ***(This action of payment is important to the instructor and will be considered in accessing the character type of a student to the instructor – This means the instructor feels that the student is responsible for his life and related associates and has the intellect to consider how his interaction can/could draw other people into his situation)***

The student agrees to waive any and all filling of law suits or complaints with any court of law or licensing board. If there is a problem that can't be resolved between the student and instructor, then the student agrees to use mediation services as the only method of solving any disputes.

Student_____DL#_____

____Phone#_____

Address_____**Referred**

by_____

(IT is the student's responsibility to give accurate contact information and update)

Signing document is interpreted as full agreement to contract as written and interpreted by instructor. If student violates contract then student agrees to pay punitive damages of $10,000 per violation as to damages to instructor are hard to access.

Student's signature

_____date_____

Instructor's

signature_____date_____

__

Cool Anger Management Program © (TM)

Designed by Joseph D. Hayes MS,LPC,NCC.

Summary of program:

The CA Program challenges clients to review their beliefs, behaviors and the resultant consequences of their anger reactions on other people, their family and society as a whole. This program draws from multiple theories to empower the client to change their life styles in order to achieve a better quality of life. The client is view afforded the respect deserving of a human being but the behavior is clearly indicative of non-acceptance. The program places responsibility directly upon the client and challenges him to change. The change is accomplished by the client as the program is merely a set of tools to assist in this change. The established groups are closed and presented in a didactic style.

Even though therapeutic change may occur, it should not be confused with therapy. Using existential gestalt and cognitive theory produces an awareness education that most clients feel comfortable enough to disclose their feelings and accept the challenge of their old beliefs and behaviors.

Goals of Program

To empower change through awareness by:

(a) Identifying faulty beliefs systems and their behavioral reactions.

(b) identifying anger triggers

(c) learning new coping skills

(d) Empowering clients to look at meaning and purpose

(e) Learning healthy and positive interactive behaviors

Outline of Program

This program consists of eight one hour and thirty min sessions. The group is didactic and is instructor driven. The class will require an individual final session of evaluation and or referrals.

I. This encounter is to assist the group in lowering defenses by doing an ice breaking activity, followed by introduction. The instructor will go over the local laws of assault, domestic violence and child abuse. The group will define the difference between rage and anger.

II. This session will focuses on belief myths and the power of belief systems. What are beliefs and how do they form? The main point at this session is to empower the client through empathy to accept responsibility for his/her behavior. Most will attempt to blame others for their physical aggression.

III. Class will view the Video" Anger Management with Joseph D. Hayes" This video is 1 hour and 20 min long. Time will be provided to process the topics as the video is stopped after each component.

IV. Continue discussion of video topics and how the clients are doing in changing their lives. Encourage all positive change. Have clients do self anger trigger identification and alternative behavioral reaction.

V. This session will be a study in emotions and how we let them affect our behaviors. Look at relationships and how they can easily become anger triggers, then lead to family stressors and parenting.

VI. This session should be focused on parenting and anger-less disciplining. How we learn parenting roles and give examples of positive discipline models of dealing with teenagers. Teenagers are important in that their development stage calls for separation from the caregiver in order to try and form an identity.

VII. Prepare clients for termination of group support. Process how we grow as a society and belief systems tend to change over the decades. Empower client to challenge himself to better his life through change.

VIII. Process how Schools, Probation, Parole, CPS, and Police are resources of assistance not enemies. Go over support resources and what to do if you feel out of control. Identify behavioral improvement areas in a group interaction. Leave the clients with feelings of accomplishment. Give unsigned certificates- So that you can see each individual on a one on one basis to provide an evaluation, referral and to sign the certificate.

Anger Management Recommendation

Levels & Fees

Level 1 Anger Management Class: This is the least restrictive; it consists of 4 hours of education. Population referred (misdemeanor assault or physical aggression charge, i.e. resisting arrest, assault by verbal threat, or terrorist threat). FEE $50

Level 2 Anger Management Class: This class consists of 4 hours classroom education, then 2 hours individual education that are directly applied to the behavior that lead to the offense and developing a plan of preventative coping skills. Population referred (Felon assault cases, maximum 2 multiple assaults or physical aggression offenses i.e. fighting, constant harassment through terrorist threat or assault with bodily injury ECT.) FEE: $100

Level 3 Individual Counseling: Treatment consist of six 30 min individual counseling sessions to address core issues related to anger and logical consequences of physical aggressive behaviors in client's life. Population referred by probation or the courts (This recommendation would be warranted after an evaluation with a supporting inventory i.e. The DVI, Domestic Violence Inventory) Fees: $25 per 30 min session = $150 and $45 for the Intake.

Level 4 and above is referred to the Batters Intervention Program (BIP)

Evaluation: Is a one on one verbal assessment interview with the offender by a Licensed Masters level counselor and an additional anger screening instrument. I.e. the DVI

Within 7 days of completing the interview with testing a written summary report with recommendations would be faxed to the probation department. Fee: $50

Test

(True or False)

1. People use anger as an excuse for striking other people?

2. You always get a second chance to make the appropriate decision or do the appropriate behavior?

3. People usually are motivated to change by frustration?

4. Money can make everyone happy?

5. People who are living a true meaning and purpose are happy?

6. One can change himself without ever being aware he has a problem?

7. Controlling ones behavior is an important part of utilizing anger management skills?

8. Forgiving always benefits the other person, not the one who forgives?

9. The main purpose of an anger outburst (tantrum, fit of aggression, etc.) by an individual is an attempt to control another person or ones surroundings?

10.   Anger is an excellent motivator?

(Multiple Choice)

1. Which word or phrase doesn't belong with what the instructor listed as the 3 steps to change?

   (a)   awareness

   (b)   plan

   (c)   support

   (d)   motivation

2. Which word or phrase doesn't belong with what the instructor demonstrated as a model of anger reaction?

   (a)   people treating one unfairly

   (b)   primary emotions of anger are fear and hurt/pain

   (c)   universal thought of being powerlessness

   (d)   anger is a secondary emotion

3. Which event can be legal trouble for an individual with anger issues?

   (a)   letting go and forgiving another person

   (b)   deescalating or intervening with a compounding thought to deescalate the emotion

(c)   cooperating with an authority figure

(d)   reacting with an aggressive behavioral reaction of holding a person until they listen

4. The best way to help any situation is

(a)   by keeping yourself in check by working on your issues

(b)   accepting other wishes and not attempting to control them

(c)   owning responsibility for ones behavior and accepting responsibility to manage ones behavior appropriately

(d)   all of the above

5. Which word or phrase doesn't belong with what the instructor discussed in stress management skills?

(a)   dealing with present events in the present, and dealing with future events by letting go until they become present events

(b)   asking what and how questions

(c)   reframing runaway thoughts with (This is only a thought intervention)

(d)   smoking a cigarette to calm your nerves

B1. Which story does not get discussed in the video by the

instructor?

(a)   the boy who cried wolf

(b)   the Indian father and his son

(c)   the monkey with a clinched fist

B2. True or False

We are attracted to other people with the same amount of

mental issues as ourselves?

Test 2

1. We are attracted to other people with the same amount of mental issues (emotional baggage) as ourselves?

2. Anger is an excellent motivator?

3. Life is always fair and gives people a second chance?

4. Frustration is often the motivation for an individual to desire change in his or her life?

5. Money is the only thing that can make people happy?

6. People using anger as the cause of them hitting other people are only making excuses?

7. Living your true meaning and purpose will allow you to experience a satisfying and happy life?

8. Forgiving someone who has done wrong to you will allow you to move on in life?

9. The main purpose of temper tantrums or anger outburst is to give the angered-out- bursting person a false sense of control?

10. Controlling your behavioral reaction is important in anger management ?

1. Which is the first step listed by Joseph D. Hayes in the three steps to change?

    a. Support

    b. Plan

    c. Awareness

    d. Motivation

2. What are the emotions that Joseph Hayes described under an anger reaction or anger?

    a love & affection

    b fear & hurt

    c universal thought of powerlessness & professional victim

    d none as anger isn't a true emotion

3. Which event can be of legal trouble for an individual with anger issues?

a. learning to let go and forgive another

b. hitting a spouse to keep him/her from leaving

c. cooperating with authority figures

d. de-escalation or intervening with a compounding thought to cool oneself down.

4. Which story does not get discussed in the anger management video?

a. the boy who cried wolf

b. the Indian father and his son

c. The monkey unwilling to let go of the banana

5. The best way to help any situation is ?

a. by keeping yourself in check by working on your own issues

b. accepting others beliefs and not attempting to change them

c. owning responsibility for ones behavior and accepting responsibility to manage ones own behavior appropriately

d. all of the above

Referral

A _____ is being referred for one or both services checked off below:

please circle

_____ The Anger Management Class. (1 day or 2 day)

_____ 6 sessions of Anger management counseling.

I agree to abide by the above recommendations and give full consent of release of confidential information (written, faxed or verbal) regarding my cooperation and progress in the anger Management services to :_____

_____

By signing below I understand and agree to above clauses and to successfully complete recommendations.

_____

Signature of client   *Date*

_____

Probation officer or witness   Date

Please contact the instructor _____ and enroll self for services. If no answer please leave confidential voice mail. Voice mail will be returned by the instructor Services will be delivered at _____ @ time_____

Bring referral slip with you

Agency name or Instructor

Phone number

Cool Anger Sign In verification

(This sheet is for counselor's records of attendance and verification of

Identification the client does not get to see this sheet)

Name_____DOB_____DL_

_____

Name_____DOB_____DL_

_____

Name_____DOB_____DL_

_____

Name_____DOB_____DL_

_____

Name_____**DOB**_____**DL**_

_____

Name_____**DOB**_____**DL**_

_____

Name_____**DOB**_____**DL**_

_____

Name_____**DOB**_____**DL**_

_____

Name_____**DOB**_____**DL**_

_____

Name_____**DOB**_____**DL**_

_____

Class   Date_____Time_____#   of   class

attendance_____

_____

Instructor

Page _____ of _____

CLASS SIGN IN ROSTER

(PLEASE GIVE ACURATE PHONE NUMBER AS THIS IS NECESSARYFOR INSTRUCTOR TO CALL IN CASE OF CLASS CANCELLATION)

PRINT

NAME:_____**PHONE**_____

_____

PRINT

NAME:_____**PHONE**_____

_____

PRINT

NAME:_____**PHONE**_____

_____

PRINT

NAME:_____**PHONE**_____

_____

PRINT

NAME:_____**PHONE**_____

_____

PRINT

NAME:_____**PHONE**_____

_____

PRINT

NAME:_____**PHONE**_____

_____

PRINT

NAME:_____**PHONE**_____

_____

PRINT

NAME:_____**PHONE**_____

_____

PRINT

NAME:_____**PHONE**_____

_____

PRINT

NAME:_____**PHONE**_____

_____

CLASS   DATE_____TIME_____#   OF

ATTENDENCE_____

Instructor_____

PAGE_____ OF _____

About the Author

Joseph D. Hayes received his Masters of Science in Community Counseling from Texas A & M Commerce in 1997. He has worked nine years as a Licensed Professional Counselor in the State of Texas. During this time he has developed multiple expertises in working with clients. His work experience began in an out-patient substance abuse treatment facility. There he received vast experience in dealing with addiction and other mental issues with both court and volunteer cliental. This experience was valuable to Mr. Hayes in that he acquired many skills that laid the foundation of his counseling practice today.

There he experienced a unique program called Intensive Intervention Diverse Program. This was a program that he was allowed to assist in group leadership, alternative activities, long term treatment vs. short term treatment therapies, alternative group techniques and individual counseling treatment of cliental. Working with this population allowed Mr. Hayes to treat many different areas of the human psyche with the supervision by Curt Pitton MA.

Mr. Hayes has also has had the privilege of serving as a counselor in an In-Patient hospital for children with mental illness. During this work experience, Mr. Hayes has performed a lot of services through his Private Practice. Today he still works performing services through his full time private practice. He self published his first book called Thera-Diet. Mr. Hayes also has a self help website at www.coolanger.com where he teaches online anger management.

He takes pride in his accomplishments, especially considering that for a couple of years he was a high school drop out. Upon getting his life back on track, he went back to school to graduate with a high school diploma at the age of twenty. Through all that he has accomplished, he expresses his most important job is raising and living with his two children as a single father. He holds many certifications, including National Certified Counselor (NCC), Anger and Depression Specialist, and is certified by the American Board of Hypnotherapy as a Clinical Hypnotherapist. If you want to contact Mr. Hayes for services, you can email him through his website at www.coolanger.com or www.counselorjoe.com.

www.ingramcontent.com/pod-product-compliance
Lightning Source LLC
Chambersburg PA
CBHW081326310526
45789CB00018B/2418